HOW BIG IS ALLAH?

CHILDREN'S FIRST QUESTIONS

Written & Illustrated by Emma Apple

For Hamza

Books by Emma Apple – Chicago IL USA

First Published by Createspace Independent Publishing 2014

Second Edition.

ISBN-13: 978-0692380970

www.emmaapple.com

BISMILLAH AR-RAHMAN AR-RAHEEM
WITH GOD'S NAME

The aim of this book is to explain the significance and greatness of Allah, the creator, using the awe of the Earth and the cosmos in which it resides.

We hope that this will help children and their families to know their creator and to look closer at the natural world to understand Him.

HOW BIG IS ALLAH?

What's the smallest thing you know?

An ant?

A snowflake?

A grain of sand?

.

Imagine how

BIG

you are compared to that!

What's the **biggest** thing you know?

A city? A Mountain? A planet?

Imagine how

Small

you are compared to that.

You are one person and there are billions of other people,
in thousands of cities around the world.

We live on a huge planet called Earth, and there are seven other planets in our solar system, many much larger than the Earth.

The planets in our solar system all orbit the Sun, which is a star that could fit a million Earths inside it.

Our Sun is one of hundreds of billions of stars in the Milky Way galaxy, many much larger.

The Milky Way galaxy is only one of the hundreds of billions of galaxies spread out in the Universe.

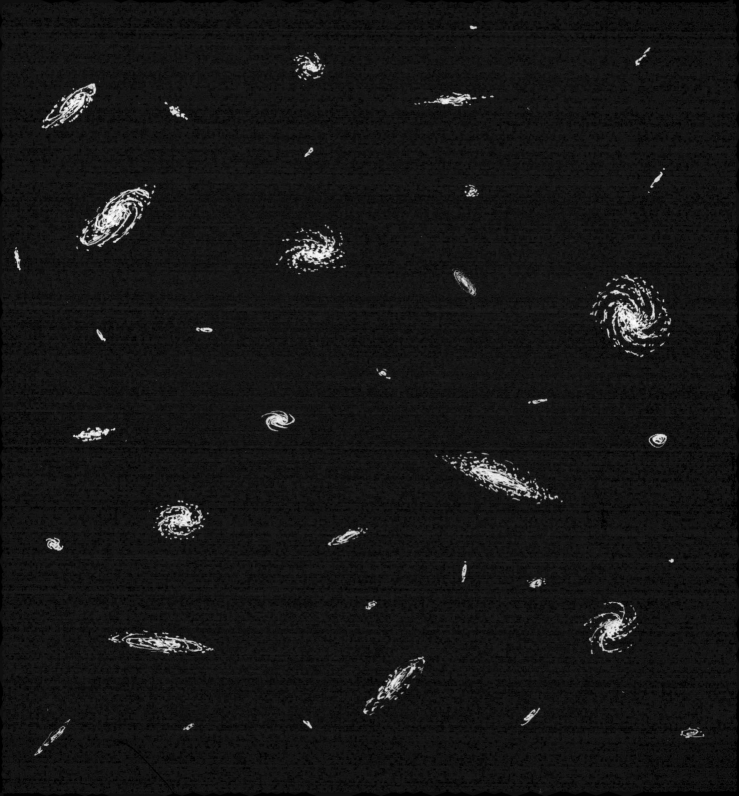

Allah created them all. From the tiniest snowflake, to you and all the things that are much bigger than you. The big Planets, the bigger Stars, the even bigger Galaxies and all the space between them.

We can't really know how big Allah is, but we can imagine how small we are and look at all the things that are bigger than us. All the planets bigger than Earth, all the stars bigger than the Sun, all the galaxies bigger than the Milky Way. All of it much bigger than we can imagine and all of it much smaller than Allah.

QUR'AN
SURAH 39 AZ-ZUMAR, AYAH 67

"They made not a just estimate of Allah such as is due to Him. And on the Day of Resurrection the whole of the earth will be grasped by His Hand and the heavens will be rolled up in His Right Hand. Glorified is He, and High is He above all that they associate as partners with Him!"

FACTS & SIZE COMPARISONS

There are approximately **7 billion** (7,000,000,000) people and more than **36 thousand** (36,000) cities on Earth right now. This number will change with time.

Jupiter, the biggest planet in our Solar System and **11 times** bigger than Earth and could fit **1,321 Earths** inside it.

The Sun is about **10 times** bigger than Jupiter and could fit about **1,300,000 Earths** inside it.

The biggest star in our Galaxy, that we know of, **VY Canis Majoris**, is about **2,000 times bigger** than our Sun.

There are estimated to be **1 to 4 hundred-billion stars** in the Milky Way galaxy. Many are average sized, like the Sun and some are much bigger.

There are estimated to be at least **100 billion galaxies** in the observable universe, many larger than the Milky Way. The biggest galaxy we know of is **IC 1101** which is about **60 times** bigger than the Milky Way.

To understand how big these numbers are:

10 tens make **a hundred (100)**.
10 hundreds make **a thousand (1,000)**.
Ten 100-thousands make **a million (1,000,000)**.
A thousand millions make **a billion (1,000,000,000)**.

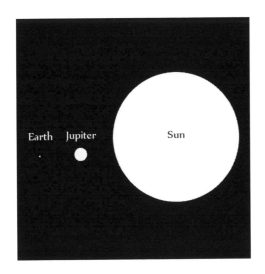

The sizes of Earth and Jupiter compared to the Sun.

The small black dot represents the position of our Solar System in the Milky Way.

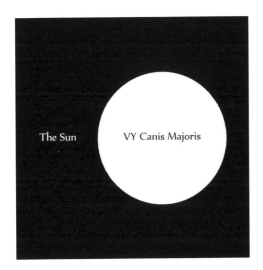

The Sun is so small compared to VY Canis Majoris it's barely visible.

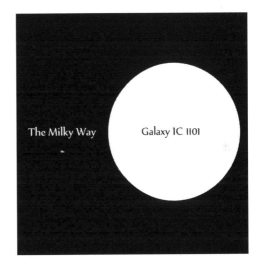

The Milky Way is tiny compared to theGalaxy IC 1101.

GLOSSARY

Allah - The One God, The Creator.

Compare - To look at how two or more things are the same.

Planet - A round object in space that orbits a star.

Solar System - A system of planets and other objects that orbit a star.

Orbit - The curved path an object takes around a star or other object.

Create - To make something exist.

Approximately - Almost but not exactly.

Estimate - To calculate something approximately.

Galaxy - A collection of stars, planets and other objects gathered together in space.

Observable - Able to be seen.

Universe - All existing things in space. Planets, Galaxies, Stars and everything that has been created.

ABOUT THE AUTHOR

Hi, I'm Emma Apple! I write and illustrate children's books for families who want unique, Science, Qur'an and Sunnah friendly bookshelves. I encourage kids to think big thoughts and expand their knowledge while accepting the limits of our understanding. I help them to grasp complex Islamic concepts using authentic Islamic sources and scientific facts.

My debut as an author-illustrator, *How Big Is Allah?* was independently published in 2014 and quickly reached #1 in the Amazon Islamic Children's category, it sold over 1,000 copies within the first year. My follow up book *How Does Allah Look?* was published in 2015 and reached #1 in the Amazon Islamic Children's category on its first day.

When I'm not writing or designing pretty things, I can be found with my husband, daughter and son, kayaking, visiting museums or reading picture books with our story-loving parrot, Ash.

FUN FACTS

1 - I'm famous for my love of yellow.
2 - Although I live in beautiful Chicago, I'm actually from New Zealand (Kia Ora!).
3 - I'm a Trekkie and have seen all the Star Trek ever made (Live long and prosper!).
4 - I own two telescopes and am a regular star (and planet) gazer.

You can find more from me online at **www.emmaapple.com**

12677806R00018

Printed in Great Britain
by Amazon.co.uk, Ltd.,
Marston Gate.